Andrew Kippis

A vindication of the protestant dissenting ministers

With regard to their late application to Parliament

Andrew Kippis

A vindication of the protestant dissenting ministers
With regard to their late application to Parliament

ISBN/EAN: 9783337131715

Printed in Europe, USA, Canada, Australia, Japan

Cover: Foto ©Suzi / pixelio.de

More available books at **www.hansebooks.com**

A

VINDICATION

OF THE

Proteſtant Diſſenting Miniſters,

With Regard to their late

APPLICATION to PARLIAMENT.

―――ſpes ſibi quiſque, ſed, hæc quam auguſta, videtis.
VIRGIL.

By ANDREW KIPPIS, D. D.

LONDON,
Printed for G. ROBINSON, in Pater-noſter-Row.
MDCCLXXII.

TO

His Grace the Duke of RICHMOND,

The Right Hon. the Earl of CHATHAM,

The Right Hon. the Earl of SHELBURNE,

AND

The Right Hon. the Lord LYTTELTON,

In grateful acknowlegement of the Reason, Eloquence, Learning, and Piety displayed by them in Support of the DISSENTERS BILL, the following Publication is humbly inscribed, by

Their most obliged,

most obedient, and

most devoted Servant,

ANDREW KIPPIS.

ADVERTISEMENT.

THOUGH the author had the honour of being one of the Committee appointed for conducting the late Application to Parliament, this performance has not been drawn up under the sanction of the Committee; and, to prevent their being, in the least degree, answerable for its faults, it has not been communicated, previous to its publication, to a single member of that body. If, therefore, in any instance, the writer has expressed himself improperly, or afforded just ground of offence, he hopes that nothing of this kind will be converted to the prejudice of a cause which he intends to serve. He takes the liberty of adding, that he thinks he hath a full right of vindicating his brethren who concur with him in sentiment, upon such principles as appear to him to be important, though they should not be exactly the same principles on which other Dissenting Ministers may proceed, who are equally well-wishers to the design of removing the Subscription required by the Toleration Act, and of obtaining Relief for Tutors and School-masters.

A VINDICATION

OF THE

Proteſtant Diſſenting Miniſters.

THE queſtion concerning the right, expediency, and utility of requiring an aſſent or ſubſcription to human articles of religion hath, for near ſixty years, been the frequent matter of debate in this country. It was largely conſidered in the celebrated controverſy, occaſioned by biſhop Hoadly's ſermon on the kingdom of Chriſt; was vigorouſly taken up and purſued in the great difference which aroſe among the Diſſenters, in 1719, and hath often been revived in the diſputes between the nonconformiſts and the clergy of the established church. But it hath never perhaps been more clearly and copiously discussed, than from the publication of the Confessional to the present time. The subject seems, indeed, to be almost exhausted in that masterly and celebrated performance; so that many persons may be disposed to think, that nothing farther need be written or read upon the question. It must, however, be acknowledged, that subsequent productions have been of no little service. They have tended still more to elucidate the matter, to spread the knowledge of it wider, and to expose the futility of all the arguments which have been urged for human tests of faith and orthodoxy. Even the writings in favour of subscription have, upon the whole, contributed to promote the contrary cause; for the authors of most of them have been so weak in their reasonings, that, in fact, they have only afforded occasion of greater triumph to their adversaries.

It seems to have been amply shewn, in the course of the controversy, that no Chri-

Christian society can have a right to impose articles of human composition on any of its members; because a requisition of this kind is contrary to the authority of our Saviour, as the lord and law-giver of his own church;—and because it is equally contrary to the principles upon which Protestantism can alone be defended, which are the liberty of private judgment, and the sufficiency of Scripture. Could it even be proved, which it never can, that such a power might be exercised without violating the precepts of the Gospel, or subverting the grounds of the Reformation from Popery; still the utility of subscriptions hath justly been called in question: nay, it hath been evinced, that they are hurtful in the highest degree; that they have been productive of endless debates, animosities, and divisions; have been one chief cause of the infidelity which prevails among the great, in almost every Christian country; and, indeed, have occasioned such a multitude of evils and miseries, as cannot be reflected upon without deeply regretting that

that mankind have not long ago been sensible of their pernicious nature, tendency, and effects.

Independent of these considerations, relative to human impositions and tests of orthodoxy in general, many of the established clergy labour under difficulties, with regard to the Thirty-nine Articles in particular. While they continue obliged to subscribe these articles, it must be impossible for them to vindicate the Christian dispensation, or to conduct their religious enquiries with the freedom and advantage which are necessary to maintain and support the cause of truth. When they engage with the enemies of revelation, they cannot defend the Gospel on its proper footing, but are embarrassed by doctrines which they may not believe to exist in the New Testament. This is certainly a great disadvantage to them in their controversies with infidels, who accordingly have gladly availed themselves of it. Indeed, the grand triumph of infidelity appears to me to arise from charging certain absurdities on the religion of Jesus,

Jesus, which are by no means to be found there; but this the clergy cannot clearly and fully prove, so long as they are hampered with tests of human composition.

The same cause must be no small embarrassment to them, in their disputes with the Papists, and their defence of the Protestant Reformation. It is true, that several of the errors, impositions, and corruptions of Popery, are condemned in the Articles; but then the authority which supports these corruptions is too much favoured by the power arrogated to the church in the Twentieth Article. The pretension to such a power, and the actual exercise of it, can never be maintained but upon principles subversive of genuine Protestantism. Until, therefore, these principles be renounced, the ministers of the establishment will often appear weak and inconsistent adversaries to the church of Rome.

Another difficulty, under which many of the clergy are laid by their subscription to the Thirty-nine Articles, arises from the Calvinistical part of the Methodists.

thodifts. It is well known how much the Methodifts of this kind triumph in the Articles, as being decifive in their favour; and can it be truly faid, that they do not triumph with reafon? I am not infenfible what learned pains have been taken to give the Articles in queftion a more liberal explication, fo as to render them confiftent with the doctrines of Arminius; but, in fuch a caufe as this, the moft able and celebrated writers muft ever bow to a Toplady and a Bowman*. It feems to be an infatuation that hath feized numbers of the clergy, who are undoubtedly Arminians, in being fo zealous for a fubfcription to Articles, which cannot be reconciled with their own fentiments. So long as this infatuation fubfifts, and fubfcription, in its prefent form, maintains its ground, the Methodifts muft increafe. Senfible of their advantage, they are of all men the moft virulent enemies to the fcheme of the peti-

---

* Two gentlemen who have lately written in defence of the Calviniftical fenfe of the Articles.

tioning

tioning clergy; as may especially be seen in the preface and notes to a late publication of Mr. Martin Madan's †.

As these, and all the other objections which may be made against subscription to human tests of religion in general, and to the Thirty-nine Articles in particular, have been so fully discussed in this inquisitive age, and so often presented to the consideration of ingenuous and thoughtful minds, it cannot be deemed surprising that they have had some influence in changing the sentiments of men; that the force of them hath been felt by many of the established clergy themselves, and that it continues to be felt more and more every day. There are numbers, no doubt, who sigh for a reformation in secret, while others have, in various forms, publicly expressed their wishes on this head. A select few have gone farther, and made an actual attempt, by petition to parliament, to obtain relief in the matter of subscription. I shall not enter into the

† His Scriptural Comment on the Thirty-nine Articles.

history of the conduct or the fate of the petition. It is well known, that the admission of it was rejected by a large majority of the House of Commons; nor will this appear extraordinary to those who reflect upon the variety of circumstances which concurred to prevent its obtaining a favourable reception.

The affair of subscription to human doctrines, though so much agitated of late years, is far from being universally or thoroughly understood. This seems to be the case with regard to a considerable part of the clergy themselves, who probably submit to the terms of ministerial conformity imposed upon them, as a thing of course, without having entertained the least doubt concerning the justice and wisdom of demanding such terms, or having made the least enquiry into the competence of the authority by which they are prescribed. Much less then can it be expected, that the laity in general should have paid attention to matters of this nature. Engaged in their business, their pleasures, their political schemes

schemes and pursuits, the members of Parliament did most of them probably think that religious concerns ought to be left to those who, by their profession, are imagined to be best acquainted with them, and therefore the House was disposed to give no countenance to a design which was supported by so few of the clerical order. The small number of the petitioners must certainly have been very prejudicial to their cause. This would have no little influence on the conduct of several of the clergy, who secretly wished well to the scheme; would blast its reputation with those who had a dislike to it; and prevent the generality of the laity from treating it with any regard.

Its originating likewise with persons of no great rank in the church must have been hurtful to it in the highest degree. In fact, it was so far from originating with, that it was opposed by the dignified clergy, and particularly by almost the whole bench of bishops, who, by their character and station, are expected to take the lead in what immediately relates to ecclesiastical matters: nor were their lordships influenced solely by disgust at the petitioners' mode of proceeding, or by the general aversion they may be thought to have to schemes of reformation, as not knowing where such schemes may end, but might imagine that too much was asked; that the precise difficulties laboured under ought to have been stated; that the articles complained of should have been specified, and not the entire abolition of subscription demanded. Subscription to some test they might consider as a fence absolutely necessary to the existence and security of religious establishments, or so important, at least, that it could not be wholly removed without danger.

But what had a great effect on many members of the legislative body was the particular idea they have formed concerning the nature of a national establishment. The public mode of religion they do not consider in a spiritual view, as what is solely to be directed by the laws

of

of Chrift and of his Gofpel, but as a certain fyftem of doctrine and worfhip, which the ftate hath adopted for its own purpofes, and for the maintenance of which a number of perfons are paid by the government. It is the opinion, therefore, of political men, that the civil magiftrate has a right of prefcribing what he pleafes with regard to the form of religion embraced and countenanced by him; that thofe who will not comply with the terms on which ecclefiaftical preferments are propofed, have no claim to them; and that fuch perfons fhould either readily perform the duty affigned them, or give up all title to the reward.

Other reafons, no doubt, concurred to prevent the fuccefs of the petitioning clergy: but thefe were probably the chief reafons by which men of the world were determined, whatever effect fpeculative and doctrinal opinions might have on the minds of individuals, and efpecially of the clergy, whether in higher or lower ftations.

Should it be asked why these things are mentioned, or what connection they have with the subject before us; I answer, that it appears to me to be of importance to mention them, because it is hence evident, that the motives for rejecting the petition of the clergy are not applicable to the situation of the Protestant Dissenting Ministers.

Without pretending to approve of the arguments which were so fatal to the petitioners, without wishing ill to their cause, many of us could not but be rejoiced to find that these arguments did not discourage an application to Parliament in our particular case. We were naturally led, both by our sentiments and situation, to pay a very diligent attention to the controversy between the dissatisfied clergy and the advocates for subscription, and to observe the progress and fate of the petitions offered to the legislature; and we saw with pleasure, that the reasons alledged for the continuance of subscription were applicable only to those who are members, and receive

receive the emoluments of a national established church. We saw, with pleasure, that none of these reasons militated against the liberty which may be claimed, and ought to be granted, under a toleration. We saw, with pleasure, that Mr. Toplady, one of the warmest defenders of the Thirty-nine Articles, had asserted, that the subscription required of the Dissenters is a real grievance, equally oppressive and absurd. We saw, with still greater pleasure, that Dr. Tucker, the ablest apologist for the church of England, had declared—" Let the ministers of Dissenting congregations, if they will choose to apply, be heartily wished a good deliverance from the burden of our subscriptions." But what gave us peculiar satisfaction was, that our case was not involved in the arguments urged against the petitioners in the House of Commons, and that it was even spoken of in a manner, which might afford a rational prospect of obtaining redress. By all these circumstances we were encouraged to hope, that we should succeed in an applicaplication to be relieved from the subscription required by the Act of Toleration: nay, such an application was highly expedient, because the peculiarity of our situation became every day more and more notorious. It was declared in several publications, it was declared in the House of Commons, that the greater part of the Dissenting Ministers had not subscribed. It was known too, that a large number of us could not possibly subscribe, and that we stood exposed to very severe penalties for our refusal. When, therefore, our danger was evidently increased, and there appeared, at the same time, a disposition to relieve us, we should have been shamefully deficient in the duty we owe to ourselves, to our posterity, and to the divine cause of religious liberty, if we had not endeavoured to obtain a legal toleration.

But though the circumstances I have mentioned encouraged an application to Parliament at this time, and we might otherwise have been contented some years longer with a state of connivance, let it not

not be imagined that we were infenfible of the infelicity of our condition, or that we did not defire and aim at procuring a deliverance from it. We were painfully confcious of our difgraceful fituation: we lamented, that, as minifters of the Gofpel, we were not under the protection of law, and could fcarcely be confidered as members of civil fociety: we felt that, in our religious capacity, whatever injuftice might be done to our perfons or characters, we were entirely deftitute of the means of redrefs. Inftances have occurred among us of men who have been obliged to defift from a legal profecution for the moft atrocious injuries, becaufe they have not qualified, and could not qualify according to the terms of the Toleration Act. It has, therefore, been not only the wifh, but the defign of many Diffenting Minifters to embrace the firft favourable opportunity of attempting to get a deliverance from the burden of fubfcription. This hath long been my own cafe; and I know that it hath been the cafe with a number of the moft refpectable of my brethren. We have often

often conversed upon the subject, and have often regretted, that when the Dissenters formerly applied for the repeal of the Test Act, they did not direct their attention and zeal to what appears to us a vastly more desirable and important object. The Test Act only excludes those who cannot comply with it, from the enjoyment of certain civil honours and preferments: the Toleration Act, if we cannot submit to its terms, legally deprives us of what we apprehend to be the common rights of human nature, and of Christianity, and subjects us to very severe penalties. We must, therefore, have been destitute of all the principles and feelings of the mental frame, if we did not regard the amendment and enlargement of such an act of parliament as a matter of unspeakable moment.

In order to shew this more particularly, it may not be improper to look back a little, to the state of things when the Toleration Act was obtained, and to the change which hath taken place in the sentiments of many of the Dissenters.

By

By the Toleration Act, Proteſtant Diſſenting Miniſters are exempted from the penal laws made againſt nonconformity, *only* on condition of their taking the oaths of allegiance and ſupremacy, making and ſubſcribing the declaration againſt Popery, and ſubſcribing alſo the Articles of the church of England, except the thirty-fourth, thirty-fifth, and thirty-ſixth, and part of the twentieth Article. Antipœdobaptiſts are farther excuſed from ſubſcribing that part of the twenty-ſeventh Article which relates to infant-baptiſm.

All Proteſtant Diſſenting Miniſters, therefore, who cannot ſubſcribe the doctrinal Articles of the church of England, are thereby excluded from the benefit of the Act of Toleration, and expoſed to the penalties of all the laws before in force againſt nonconforming miniſters. " They are not to come or be, unleſs in paſſing upon the road, within five miles of any city, or town corporate, or borough that ſends burgeſſes to parliament; or within five miles of any pariſh, town, or place where they have taken upon them to preach;

preach; upon forfeiture, for every such offence, of the sum of forty pounds; one third to the king, another third to the poor of the parish, and another to him that shall sue for it;" and if such person keep a school, he shall forfeit, likewise, for every such offence, " forty pounds; and any two justices of the peace may, upon oath made of any of these offences, commit such offender for six months, without bail or main-prize." They are also liable, on conviction upon oath of two witnesses, before one or more justices of the peace, of having preached; for the first offence, to a penalty of twenty pounds; and for every such offence afterwards, to a penalty of forty pounds. And by another act, for every such offence they are liable to suffer three months imprisonment in the common jail, without bail or main-prize. And every time they administer the Lord's supper, they are liable to a penalty of one hundred pounds; one moiety to go to the king, another moiety to be divided between the poor of the parish, and such

person

person or persons as shall sue for the same by action of debt, bill, plaint, or information, in any court of record, wherein no essoign, protection, or wager of law shall be allowed.

To these severe penalties, such Protestant Dissenting Ministers as have not subscribed the Articles before-mentioned, are exposed: and, in the last case, a very ample reward is proposed to every prosecutor, out of the forfeiture incurred; and the prosecution is, at the same time, made as easy as possible *.

This is the situation we are left in by the Act of Toleration. It is only by complying with the subscription enjoined by it, that we can legally be permitted to conduct the worship of the God and Father of mercies in that manner which we think agreeable to the dictates of truth, Scripture, and conscience; and the penalties to which we are otherwise subject are such, that every ingenuous and

---

* See the Case of the Protestant Dissenting Ministers and Schoolmasters.

liberal man muſt ſtart back with horror at the recital of them. Nay, they are penalties which even bigotry itſelf ſcarce dares to call for the exaction of, in the preſent age.

There is another circumſtance, of the greateſt importance, for which relief is not provided by the Act of Toleration, even upon any terms. The right of educating our children, according to our own views of what will be moſt conducive to their temporal and eternal felicity, is one of the deareſt rights of human nature; one of the laſt privileges which a man would be willing to give up, who is endued with the feelings of parental affection, and the principles of piety, integrity, and honour. But this is a privilege to which the Proteſtant Diſſenters have no *legal* title. By the cruel laws of king Charles the ſecond, every nonconformiſt, of every kind, is diſabled from acting in the capacity of a tutor or ſchoolmaſter, and proſecutions cannot be diverted without conſiderable trouble and expence. This is a caſe that includes the Laity, as well

well as the Ministers, and which does indeed speak loudly for itself*.

Many persons will, without doubt, be ready to wonder how it could possibly come to pass, that the Toleration Act should be so very defective. But this must be sought for in the principles and spirit of the times.

At the glorious period of the Revolution, religious liberty, in its due extent, was, comparatively speaking, very imperfectly understood. Experience had, indeed, instructed the nation, in the evil consequences which had arisen from persecuting the nonconformists. It was found that the disunion and animosities of the Protestants were hurtful to the common cause, and added strength to the schemes and enterprizes of the Papists. It was necessary, therefore, to unite the former together; and the sincere and zealous concurrence of the Dissenters, in promoting the late change of

---

* See the Case of the Protestant Dissenting Ministers and Schoolmasters.

govern-

government, was an additional reason for treating them with favour. King William was desirous of conferring greater marks of distinction upon them than a bare toleration; but this was the whole that could be obtained, and it was even debated, whether the Toleration should be allowed for more than a certain number of years. When its permanency was disputed, it cannot be surprizing that it did not in other respects go upon enlarged principles. The truth of the case was, that the nation was not yet sufficiently enlightened upon the subject. Toleration was not, indeed, forgotten among the important topics which were discussed during the time of the civil war: liberty of conscience was pleaded for by the independents; and Dr. Owen, among others, wrote in its favour: but a due regard was not paid to their principles and reasonings. The obnoxiousness of the men to the two great parties of Episcopalians and Presbyterians, had prevented the easy reception of any doctrine which came from them,

them, however juft or generous it might in itfelf be. Locke's excellent Letters were but now beginning to make their appearance; and it was a long time before the admirable fentiments contained in them came to be generally diffufed. It was not doubted, but that perfons, who entertained certain doctrines called heretical, were by no means fit to be tolerated; and the principal part of the nonconformifts, notwithftanding the long perfecution they had endured, had not yet divefted themfelves of this perfuafion. They did not think of queftioning the right of the civil magiftrate to impofe fubfcription to human tefts of faith and orthodoxy: they even believed it to be his duty to reftrain what were apprehended to be fundamental errors and herefies: and though fome minifters might entertain more liberal views of things, they were glad to accept of liberty of confcience on fuch terms as were offered, and could then be obtained. Thefe terms were the lefs difagreeable to them, as being Calvinifts, or nearly Calvinifts, they had

had scarce any difficulties with regard to the doctrinal Articles; but could chearfully subscribe them, as containing their own real opinions*.

But since the period we have been speaking of, a great, a just, and important revolution hath taken place in the sentiments of the Protestant Dissenters upon these subjects. Most of the Dissenting Clergy ground their separation from the establishment on principles that differ, in some considerable respects, from those upon which their ancestors proceeded. We do, indeed, agree with the original Puritans in the desire they had to discard entirely the corruptions of popery, and to restore Christian worship to the simplicity and purity of the Gospel standard. We applaud their conduct in

---

* Some expressions in the Articles appearing dubious to Mr. Baxter, he drew up a brief explication, which he gave in for his sense at the time of his subscription, and many of his brethren concurred with him in giving the same explication. It is inserted in Calamy's Abridgment of the Life of Baxter. Vol. I. p. 469—476.

resisting

refifting fo firmly the unfcriptural terms of conformity impofed upon them, and we retain a grateful remembrance of their integrity and fortitude. We have, in particular, the utmoft veneration for the memory of thofe two thoufand men, who, in the year 1662, nobly facrificed their preferments and their fubfiftence for the caufe of God and a good confcience. But, at the fame time, we do not diffent fo much as they did, on account of fcruples with regard to certain ceremonies, habits, and modes of government and difcipline; nor do we diffent folely on account of fome objections which may be urged againft the Liturgy and Offices of the church of England. It is true, that we have our difficulties on thefe heads, and feveral of them are of a ferious and weighty nature. Several of them are fuch as, while they fubfift, muft for ever keep us at a diftance from conformity. But befides the particular objections we have to a number of the rites and forms of the national worfhip, we found our diffent on what appear to us to be moft important general reafons. We

E   diffent,

dissent, because we deny the right of any body of men, whether civil or ecclesiastical, to impose human tests, creeds, or articles; and because we think it our duty, not to submit to any such authority, but to protest against it, as a violation of our essential liberty to judge and act for ourselves in matters of religion. We dissent, because we apprehend that the church of England, in the requisition of a subscription to her doctrines and ceremonies, claims and exercises a power which we look upon as derogatory to the honour of our great Master, the sole legislator in his own kingdom; and because we believe ourselves bound, as his professed disciples and followers, to stand up for his honour in opposition to all encroachments.

Independently, therefore, of the truth of the Thirty-nine Articles, the generality of Dissenting Ministers object to the imposition of these Articles. Persuaded as they are of the sufficiency of Scripture, and the liberty every one ought to have of following the guidance of his own conscience

science in religious concerns, they will not subscribe to formularies, which they themselves believe, when such formularies are pressed upon them by an incompetent and usurped authority. It is their fixed principle, that the writings of the Old and New Testament, are the only rule of faith and practice; and, therefore, were they, in matters of religion, and when asking for a Toleration, to go any farther in their submission to the civil magistrate, than to make this declaration of their Christian and Protestant character, being the specific character in which they appear before the legislature, they would be guilty of an act of treason against their Lord and Saviour. How far they may be well founded in these sentiments is not my business, at present, to determine. Their views of things may appear to some too refined, to others wholly fanciful; but that has no relation to the question before us. These opinions are matters of conscience, and the persons who entertain them ought to be indulged, ought to be tolerated, provided they are peaceable members of the community.

That this is a faithful account of the state of things among the Proteſtant Diſſenters is evident not only from the general ſtrain of their late publications, but from two facts which are worthy of the reader's notice. The firſt is the ſolemn declaration of a majority of the Diſſenting Clergy, in the year 1719, when a controverſy having ariſen on the ſubject of the Trinity, a meeting of the miniſters in and about London was held at Salters-hall, to conſider of *Articles of Advice for Peace*, to be ſent to their brethren and to the congregations in other places. At this meeting, it was propoſed to inſert in the Advices the firſt Article of the Church of England, and the Anſwers to the fifth and ſixth Queſtions in the Aſſembly's Catechiſm; but the requiſition was nobly withſtood by the more enlightened part of the body, and it was carried, by a majority of fifty-ſeven againſt fifty-three, *That no human compoſitions or interpretations of the doctrine of the Trinity ſhould be made*

made a part of the Articles of Advice. It is observable, that all of these fifty-seven ministers were believers, and most of them zealous asserters of the commonly-received opinions with regard to the Trinity; but they thought it their duty to stand up for the liberty wherewith Christ has made us free, and to enter their protest against the yoke of human impositions. It is much to the honour of this small but illustrious majority, that it appears to be the first instance in which a body of clergymen publicly asserted and maintained the cause of religious freedom, and the sacred rights of conscience*.

That the fifty-seven ministers were real believers of the common opinion concerning the Trinity, is evident from the following passage, which is taken from the Letter written by them, in conjunction with sixteen more of their brethren, accompany-

* The author doth not intend to cast any reflection upon the subscribing ministers, who were undoubtedly persons of distinguished piety, and acted from a strong sense of duty: but he must be allowed to give the preference, in his esteem, to their more enlightened brethren.

ing the Advices they had agreed to send to Exeter.

"We freely declare, that we utterly disown the Arian doctrine, and sincerely believe the doctrine of the blessed *Trinity*, and the *proper* divinity of our Lord Jesus Christ, which we apprehend to be clearly revealed in the Holy Scriptures; but are far from condemning any who appear to be with us in the main, though they should chuse not to declare themselves in other than Christian terms, or not in ours."

This Declaration they farther explained thus:

"The human words *Trinity* and *proper divinity*, in this *Declaration* of our faith, are used only to notify the things we speak of; and we do not presume, in the way of *test*, to go into any particular explanations of those things, either in our *own*, or *other* mens words: but for that we refer to the Holy Scriptures, whence it may appear, that we take the Scripture account of those things to be
the

the *best* and fittest we can use on such occasions."

The fourth article of the Advices was as follows:

" If, after all, a public hearing be insisted on, we think the Protestant principle, that *the Bible is the only and the perfect rule of faith*, obliges those who have the case before them, not to condemn any man upon the authority of human decisions, or because he consents not to human forms or phrases: but then only is he to be censured, *as not holding the faith necessary to salvation*, when it appears that he contradicts, or refuses to own, the *plain and express declarations of Holy Scripture*, in what is there made necessary to be believed, and in matters there solely revealed. And we trust that all will treat the servants of their common Lord, as they who expect the final decision at his appearing*."

Though,

---

* The only surviving person of the non-subscribing ministers is Mr. Henry Read, a gentleman whom a long life of irreproachable piety and distinguished usefulness hath rendered truly venerable. He is the father of the present body of Protestant Dissenting Ministers, is in the

Though, in 1719, the Diffenting Ministers were almoſt equally divided in their opinions concerning human teſts, the ſituation of things is now happily changed, much for the better in this reſpect, as will be manifeſt from the ſecond fact I have to produce. It is well known, that Dr. Furneaux hath ſtated and defended the preſent principles of the Diſſenters upon the enlarged grounds I have mentioned, and not upon ſcruples relative to particular articles or doctrines. That he hath truly ſtated and defended their preſent principles admits of no doubt, from the thanks which, at the motion of one of our moſt ancient, eminent, and reſpectable miniſters*, were unanimouſly voted to him, by the general body of the three denominations of Preſbyterians, Independents, and Baptiſts, for his Letters to the Hon. Mr. Juſtice Blackſtone. I ſhall beg leave to lay before the public the minutes of the proceedings with regard to this affair.

the eighty-ſeventh year of his age, and expreſſed his entire approbation of the late application to Parliament.

* Dr. Prior.

" At

"At a meeting of the general body of the Proteſtant Diſſenting Miniſters, of the three denominations, in and about the cities of London and Weſtminſter, held at the Library, in Red-crofs-ſtreet, April 16, 1771.

"Agreed, at the motion of Mr. Prior, that the thanks of this body be given to the Rev. Dr. Furneaux, for the great ſervice he has done to the cauſe of religious liberty in general, and for his able defence of the rights and privileges of Proteſtant Diſſenters in particular, in his excellent Letters to the Honourable Mr. Juſtice Blackſtone; and that the chairman do preſent the thanks of this body to the Rev. Dr. Furneaux, in their name with the firſt convenient opportunity."

"At a meeting of the general body, Nov. 20, 1771.

"Reported, by Mr. Pitts, chairman of the laſt meeting of the general body, that he had, according to order, returned the thanks of this body to the Rev. Dr. Furneaux, and received a letter from the doctor, which was read.

"Agreed,

" Agreed, at the motion of Dr. Harris That Dr. Furneaux's letter to Mr. Pitts be, with Mr. Pitts's leave, transcribed into this book; of which letter the following is a copy.

" Reverend and dear sir,

" I am extremely sorry, that I did not happen to be at home, when you did me the favour of a visit this morning. I hope I shall have the pleasure of your company on some other occasion.

" Your two last favours, the one acquainting me with the resolution of the general body of the Protestant Dissenting Ministers, in and about the cities of London and Westminster, with respect to my Letters to Mr. Justice Blackstone, and the other inclosing that Resolution, as it stands on the Minutes, conveyed to me an honour of which I had not the least apprehension, and of the value of which I am very sensible. This unanimous approbation of my brethren of all denominations is, in the present case, the more agreeable

agreeable to me, as it is a clear proof that I have not, in any manner, misrepresented the principles of the Protestant Dissenters on the head of religious liberty. My aim was only to do them justice; and that so respectable a body, who must know their own sentiments, and cannot be supposed ignorant of those which prevail amongst the Dissenting Ministers and people in general, have declared their opinion that I have not done them injustice, gives me, I own, no small satisfaction. All beyond this I esteem (as I ought) to be a demonstration of their candour and friendship. I acknowledge, with thanks, the very obliging manner, in which you, sir, as chairman, have acquainted me with the sentiments of the body, and am

" Your very affectionate brother,

" and obedient humble servant,

" Clapham, April   " PHILIP FURNEAUX."
" 25th, 1771.

Such then, as I have stated them, may now be considered the general principles of the Dissenting Ministers; so that however firmly they may believe the doctrinal Articles of the Church of England, they cannot but be averse to having a subscription to them imposed by human authority, and must sincerely desire an enlargement of the Toleration Act. It may, perhaps, be a matter of curiosity to know how such an alteration hath been brought about in the sentiments of the Dissenters; and it must chiefly be ascribed to the particular attention which hath been paid to the subject of religious liberty, from the period of the Revolution to the present time. Mr. Locke's admirable Letters on Toleration, had, no doubt, a considerable effect on the minds of thoughtful and philosophical persons. But the circumstance which much contributed to open the eyes of Dissenting Ministers, was Dr. Calamy's Introduction to the second volume of his Defence of Moderate Nonconformity. From henceforward, the controversy between the
Church

Church of England and the Dissenters, was placed, in part, on a new footing. The solid and manly reasonings of Dr. Calamy have been confirmed and pursued through all their consequences. It is an undoubted fact, that his arguments were approved of by Mr. Locke; and bishop Hoadly himself appears to have been enlightened by them. It is certain, at least, that he availed himself of the same method of reasoning in his subsequent writings: and from the time of the Hoadlian controversy to the present day, the objections to the exercise of human authority in matters of religion; and the arguments in favour of the right of private judgment, the sufficiency of Scripture, and the sole dominion of Christ over his Church, have been exhibited in such a variety of unanswerable performances, that the man who did not ground his separation from the establishment, chiefly upon these considerations, would scarce be thought worthy the name of a Dissenter. The Presbyterians in particular, with regard to their notions of ecclesiastical power

power and government, are a different set of men from the Presbyterians of the last century. The English Presbyterians of this age have discarded all ideas of parochial sessions, classes, provincial synods, and general assemblies. They disclaim all coercive jurisdiction in spiritual concerns; and believe, that every distinct and separate congregation ought to be the sole director of its religious affairs, without being controulable by, or accountable to any other earthly authority. In short, except their denial of any scriptural distinction between the office of a Bishop and a Presbyter, and their uniting in the same mode of worship, they retain little of Presbyterianism, properly so called, but the name.

I cannot avoid stopping a moment to observe, that the alterations produced in the sentiments of religious sects, while the original denominations are continued, ought to be particularly noticed by ecclesiastical writers; for, unless a considerable degree of attention be paid to these things, the accounts which are given of the different parties

parties that have divided the church of Christ, must be very confused, imperfect, and diffatisfactory. I have often had occasion to remark, that even some of the best church historians have fallen into errors in this respect.

But though, from what hath been alleged, it is apparent that the generality of Dissenting Ministers, however strongly they may believe in the particular doctrines contained in the Thirty-nine Articles, must object to the terms required by the Toleration Act, and wish to be exempted from a compliance with them; it cannot, at the same time, be denied, and it ought not to be concealed, that a number of persons among us, dislike, in many respects, the doctrines themselves; and, therefore, have a powerful additional reason for desiring and soliciting the removal of subscription.

A course of time hath produced a great alteration in the sentiments of several of our brethren. Doctrines, formerly disputed by few, have, during the present century, been freely called in question; and

and opinions have been entertained very different from those of Calvin and Athanasius. Whether men have acted right in rejecting the dogmas of the spirited reformer, and the zealous saint, is of no importance to determine. The only question is, whether those who do not believe the doctrinal Articles, have not the same reasonable claim to indulgence as their predecessors had, with regard to the Articles more immediately relative to ceremonies, discipline, and church authority: and here, if the matter be considered with reference to the great object which political government hath in view, it will easily be decided. Supposing a person should happen to embrace what are deemed the particular and distinguishing tenets of Arminius, Arius, or Socinus, what hath all this to do with the welfare of the state? The business of the magistrate, as hath unanswerably been shewn by Mr. Locke, is to take care of the temporal, and not of the eternal interests of mankind. With regard to the things which concern our future life, we are accountable to God alone,

alone, and to our great Lord and Master Jesus Christ. With respect to religious concerns, the civil power ought to go no farther, in the way of restraint and punishment, at least, than to prevent different sects from injuring each other; and to take care that they do not, on any pretence, disturb the public tranquility. It will readily, I imagine, be granted, that Arminians may be valuable members of society, and worthy of its protection; because, notwithstanding the Calvinistical structure of the Thirty-nine Articles, the majority of the clergy are professedly Arminians: and why may not Arians and Socinians be equally valuable members of society, and equally worthy of its protection? I speak here solely of them in a civil capacity, the only capacity with which the state is properly and justly concerned. What is there in the opinions of these men, which disqualifies them from being good subjects, or enjoying a legal security? Do they advance doctrines subversive of the general peace and safety? Nothing of this kind can be charged upon them, with the

the least shadow of reason or justice. If they hold any sentiments that may be supposed to be highly erroneous, or even dangerous to their salvation, that is a matter of which the supreme Being alone hath a right to take cognizance, and which must be determined at his tribunal. Let not men, therefore, presume to claim a jurisdiction over the consciences of their fellow-creatures, but remember that God hath committed all judgment to his Son.

It appears, then, from what hath been advanced, that if there be Dissenting Ministers who do not believe several of the doctrinal Articles of the church of England, as there undoubtedly are, they ought not to be obliged to subscribe; because, without doing it, they have a natural right to Toleration. The conduct of the state, and of the public, for more than fifty years, hath already determined that they have such a right. Though it be a known fact, that many of the Dissenting Clergy have not submitted, and cannot submit, to the subscription required ed of them by law, they have been allowed to go on quietly in their religious employments; and the experience of half a century hath proved, that the lenity shewn to them hath been of no prejudice to the community. The change of their situations and sentiments is such, that, if the indulgence they have hitherto met with be withdrawn, they must be exposed to all the persecutions which disgraced the reign of king Charles the second. But the continuation of the indulgence doth not depend merely on the equity and moderation of government; it depends, likewise, on the equity and moderation of every individual in this country: it depends on there not being a single person in the nation, who can be prevailed upon to disturb us, either by the dictates of bigotry, or the stimulations of avarice. Why then should bands be suffered to remain about us, that are confessedly needless and useless; and which, though hanging loose around us at present, may, at the pleasure of any one, be drawn so close as to become very painful, and even

even intolerable? It is not surely desirable for penal laws to subsist, which, at best, are unnecessary; and which, if carried into execution, must be productive of flagrant injustice and cruelty. The permitting of them to be continued, when a proper application is made for their repeal, is contrary to every principle of a wise and equitable legislation.

Those persons, who think that we ought to have rested satisfied with the connivance so long granted us, do not appear to me to have considered the matter with due attention. A state of connivance is greatly inferior to a state of legal security. Will any one assert, that the liberties and privileges we enjoy as Britons, are not infinitely more valuable, as founded in law, than if they depended entirely on the character and disposition of the sovereign, whatever probability there might be of a succession of wise, just, and merciful princes? It is the glory of the British constitution, that it is built on more solid foundations than the good intentions of men, and the accidental tem-

temper of ages. The very confcioufnefs of enjoying the moſt invaluable benefits only by the connivance of our fellow-creatures muſt be grating to every generous mind. Befides, who can anfwer for it, that a ſtate of connivance ſhall never be interrupted? It is poſſible at leaſt, if not probable, that other men and other times may ſucceed to thofe we have now the happinefs of beholding; and, therefore, I cannot but think, that the Diffenting Miniſters acted wifely, in endeavouring to improve what they believed a favourable opportunity for obtaining a legal fecurity to themfelves and their poſterity, in the exercife of that liberty of confcience, which they deem the moſt important and facred bleſſing that Providence can put into their hands.

In the late application to Parliament, we grounded our hopes of fuccefs not only on the circumſtances which I have already mentioned, but upon a variety of additional confiderations. We were confcious that we lived under a prince of the Brunfwick line; a prince, with regard to whom, it would

would be shameful to assert, that he is not as ready to defend, and even to enlarge the just and reasonable privileges of his subjects as any of his royal predecessors. We believed that administration could have no objection to a request that was most equitable in itself, and which might have been granted without the shadow of injury, danger, or disturbance to the public. With regard to the members of both Houses of Parliament, we trusted that their wisdom and moderation would dispose them to rescue the Statute Book from penal acts which are a disgrace to it, and to give relief to a peaceable body of men, who did not deserve to be marked out by the laws, as criminals, hateful to the state. As to the bishops in particular, we had been taught to expect every thing from the mild and candid spirit of the present bench. We knew that the sentiments of all ranks of men were, for the most part, averse to restraint and severity in matters of religion; and we were not ignorant that TOLERATION had lately lifted up her voice so loudly in Europe, as to be heard

heard and attended to, even in arbitrary and popish governments.

Encouraged by such a number of flattering appearances, we ventured, with all humility and respect, to lay our case before the Legislature, and to solicit an enlargement of the Toleration Act. The final result of the application is well known. Our bill, after having passed the House of Commons, was rejected in the House of Peers by a large majority. But notwithstanding the mortification of our defeat, there are some circumstances which we can reflect upon with pleasure, as not a little honourable to our cause. It is undoubtedly a great credit to the bill, that it went through the Lower House with so general a concurrence. The free and unbiassed voice of the representatives of the people was strongly in its favour; and that is a matter which must appear important in the public eye, and will, we trust, not be destitute of valuable effects.*

The

* The motion for leave to bring in the bill was made by sir Henry Hoghton, a gentleman of irreproachable integrity, of a cultivated understanding, and a liberal mind;

The reasonableness and equity of our petition were well debated and nobly supported in both houses; and none will dare to deny, that with us were the most able, judicious, and eloquent speakers. I proceed not to particular names, because I am incapable of doing justice to their characters and merit; but they are such as will carry down the history of our application with honour even to the remotest

mind; and it was seconded by Sir George Savile, whose eminent abilities and character are universally known and acknowledged. The speakers in favour of the bill, at different times, besides the above-mentioned gentlemen, were Frederick Montagu, Esq. the Right Hon. George Onslow, Esq. the Hon. Constantine John Phipps, Esq. Edmund Burke, Esq. the Right Hon. Lord Viscount Clare, Jeremiah Dyson, Esq. John Sawbridge, Esq. Sir Joseph Mawbey, Bart. the Hon. Stephen Fox, Esq. Charles Wolfranç Cornwall, Esq. Sir William Meredith, Bart. Colonel Jennings, James Harris, Esq. Richard Whitworth, Esq. the Right Hon. George Rice, Esq. and the Right Hon. Lord John Cavendish. These are names which do honour to our cause. Many other members, of the most distinguished capacities and merit, were ready to have spoken in its support; but the opposition to the bill in the House of Commons was so feeble as to render a farther display of reason and eloquence totally unnecessary.

times.

times. We had the peculiar satisfaction of knowing that the two greatest of the law lords † divided for the commitment of the bill; an evident proof that they considered the principle it went upon as the proper object of legislation, and the cause it was intended to support as the cause of equity and good government. On the one side were truth, reason, eloquence, justice, and religion; on the other—PUDET HÆC OPPROBIA—DICI POTUISSE—most of the temporal peers, and ALL THE BISHOPS.*

But notwithstanding these pleasing and honourable circumstances, our adversaries have abundant reason for rejoicing. It might, however, have been expected that they would have satisfied themselves with privately exulting at our defeat; but that, it seems, was not a sufficient display of their triumph. In the pride of parliamentary victory, they have thought proper to draw out the pen against us, and to attack

† Lord Mansfield and Lord Camden.

* All the bishops who were present in the House of Peers, or who ordered their proxies to be given in opposition to the bill.

us, with all the formality of ecclesiastical pedantry, upon the MATTER, the MANNER, and the TIME of our application. It was not, perhaps, wise in them, to move a controversy which might otherwise have lain dormant. If we had been permitted to return quietly to our ministerial labours and studies, we might have waited in silence for a more favourable opportunity of urging our cause. But since we are wantonly provoked to the contest, let us engage in it with alacrity and temper, and attend somewhat more particularly to the MATTER, the MANNER, and the TIME of our application.

As to the MATTER of our application, THAT should seem to be sufficiently vindicated by what hath already been offered. The reasons for it were so strong and weighty, that it might have been expected every candid person would acknowledge that we had just cause for having recourse to legislature. What could be a more proper request to legislature than to be delivered from a subjection to laws, which, confessedly, cannot be put into execution? But since particular difficulties

culties have been started upon this head, it may not be amiss to pay them some degree of attention.

One objection then, which hath been urged against the late application of the Dissenting Ministers, is drawn from the Act of Toleration, as if that act could not admit of improvement. It is, it seems, a fundamental law of the state, which hath fixed bounds for ever to the exercise of liberty of conscience, and determined what doctrines should always be held by the professors of Christianity, of every denomination, in this country. But what foundation can there be for such a representation of things ? That toleration is essential to every well-formed system of government will most readily be granted; but that a partial and defective toleration cannot be extended, is surely a strange position.

We have shewn that the Act of Indulgence, which passed in the beginning of the reign of king William and queen Mary, evidently partook of the imperfect ideas of the times; that men were not, at that period, enlightened enough to grant a greater degree of religious freedom; and that the principal part of the Diffenters did not wifh to be exempted from doctrinal fubfcriptions. But what right had the legiflators of that age fo abfolutely to fettle the limits of toleration, as to fay, HITHERTO SHALT THOU GO, AND NO FARTHER? If THEY thought that it was neceffary to fubfcribe certain tefts, in order to be admitted to any liberty of worfhip, they had no authority to determine, that fuch tefts fhould always be confidered as effential to the enjoyment of the public protection. The confining of indulgence to the belief of particular tenets, or to a compliance with human articles, was, at that time, contrary to the principles of reafon, legiflation, Chriftianity, and Proteftantifm; but to have pretended to fix thefe terms for future periods, fo that it fhould not be in the power of fucceeding generations to alter or reverfe them, would have been abfurd in the higheft degree. It would have been both contrary to the principles upon which ALONE the Reformation

mation could be justified, and to the very design and spirit of the Toleration Act. Its intention was, to give relief to such scrupulous consciences as then existed; when, therefore, other scruples of conscience arise among men, who are upright and peaceable members of the community, it is agreeable to the real genius and meaning of that act, that such cases should be provided for. I should wish to be informed, how long this idea of its being a pactum conventum, never, in any respect, to be improved, hath been started. I have not before met with it in the course of my reading, and believe that it hath not been advanced by any gentlemen learned in the law. It seems to be, evidently, an EPISCOPAL invention, produced, without the colour of reason or equity, to prevent the success of the late application. However high and respectable, therefore, may be the rank of the persons from whom the notion proceeded; and however largely it may have lately been insisted upon; I beg leave to dismiss it with contempt, as big with absurdity and falsehood;

hood; as repugnant to every juſt idea of the nature of Chriſtianity, the end of civil government, and the reaſonable demands of Toleration.

Another thing, which hath been much inſiſted upon, is the vagueneſs of the declaration propoſed to the legiſlature, in the room of the ſubſcription heretofore required; but in no reſpect can it be proved to be ſo. "WE DECLARE, AS IN THE PRESENCE OF ALMIGHTY GOD, THAT WE BELIEVE THAT THE HOLY SCRIPTURES OF THE OLD AND NEW TESTAMENT CONTAIN A REVELATION OF THE MIND AND WILL OF GOD, AND THAT WE RECEIVE THEM AS THE RULE OF OUR FAITH AND PRACTICE." Now what can be a more explicit declaration of our Chriſtian and Proteſtant principles? To aſſert, as hath been aſſerted, that it may be made by a Deiſt, a Mohammedan, or a Papiſt, is very ſurprizing. Can an infidel ſay, that he believes that the holy Scriptures, of the Old and New Teſtament, contain a revelation of the mind and will of God, and that he receives them

them as THE rule of HIS faith and practice? Can a Mohammedan, whose standard of doctrine and worship is the Koran, pretend that the holy Scriptures of the Old and New Testament are THE rule of HIS faith and practice? Or can the Roman Catholic, who holds the infallibility of the pope, or of general councils, and who maintains the authority of the traditions of the church, declare that the Scriptures are THE rule of HIS faith and practice? It is impossible, that any of these persons could subscribe the declaration with truth. They could not do it, consistently with the principles they profess to embrace. In short, by this declaration, Dissenting Ministers do, BONA FIDE, proclaim, that they are Christians and Protestants, and may safely appeal to the great Searcher of hearts for the integrity of their conduct. With regard to any charge, or insinuation to the contrary, I beg leave to borrow of Lord Chatham the best words that can be used upon the subject: "Who-
"ever thinks so, thinks uncharitably;
"and whoever says so, without proof,
"is guilty of defamation."

With regard to Popery, the Diffenting Minifters are ready, likewife, to fubfcribe the Declaration required by law; to which may be added, that they CHEARFULLY take the oaths of allegiance and fupremacy, and are defirous of giving all reafonable fecurity to government, for their behaving in a manner that fhall juftly entitle them to its protection. Nothing more, therefore, ought to be required; and with refpect to matters of doctrine, they can go no farther in their fubmiffion to the civil magiftrate, than they have already offered to do. Were they to go farther, they would, as hath been fhewn above, depart from their profeffed principles, as Chriftians, Proteftants, and Proteftant Diffenters. Were they to go farther, they would break the bond which holds them together, and defert the caufe of truth and of God, in which they are united.

Two or three of our brethren have objected to the Declaration ITSELF, affented to by the committee, not as difbelieving it, but as a demand which the magiftrate has

no

no right to make, and as a concession which ought not to be submitted to on our part. In answer to these gentlemen, I beg leave to observe, that my idea of Toleration is as large as theirs can possibly be, and that I wish to see it granted in its full extent. Religion is the business of the heart, and to be efficacious must be voluntary. Religion, in every form of it which is consistent with the safety of the state, has an unlimited title to indulgence. I do not, therefore, think that liberty of conscience ought to be confined to Christianity; nor do I think, that the magistrate hath, properly and strictly, a right to interpose in religious matters, so as to lay ANY restraint upon, or to prescribe ANY test, to those who behave as peaceable subjects. I consider the Declaration as needless, with regard to Dissenting Ministers; and am fully persuaded, that they have a just and unexceptionable claim to be tolerated without it. In the sixth year of the reign of king George the first, a Toleration was granted to the Dissenters in Ireland, on the terms only of subscribing the Decla-

I ration

ration againſt Popery, and taking the oaths of allegiance and ſupremacy; and this appears to be a ſecurity to the ſtate, which is abundantly ſufficient. Its ſufficiency has been proved, by the experience of more than half a century; during which, not the leaſt diſadvantage hath ariſen to government from granting liberty of conſcience on ſuch generous principles. We know, too, that the Epiſcopalians have been tolerated in Scotland upon the like terms. For theſe reaſons, I ſhould be better pleaſed if we could be admitted to the benefit of the Toleration Act, upon the ſame conditions which are annexed to it in Ireland; and I ſhould have deemed it abſolutely my duty, to refuſe conceding to the Declaration of the bill, if it had been apprehended, that it would have left any ſcrupulous brother in a worſe ſtate than he was in before. But as the committee were perſuaded that this would not have been the caſe, and underſtood that ſome declaration was expected, they were deſirous of obtaining an important addition to religious liberty, in a way which they believed ed consistent with the universal principles of the Dissenters. Let it be remembered, that it was not the business of the Dissenting Ministers, in their late application, to take upon them the cause of all mankind, however sincerely they might wish the most unlimited indulgence to the sacred rights of conscience. They were not constituted deputies of the whole human race, but appeared in the particular character of Protestant Dissenting Ministers, and asked the relief which was wished for in that particular situation. Could they, therefore, really object, or could they expect that any of their brethren would object to their declaring the distinguishing and universal principles of the Dissenting Clergy? Could they refuse to tell their names? Could they hesitate, for the sake of receiving an important benefit, to confess a truth we all glory in, THAT WE BELIEVE THAT THE HOLY SCRIPTURES OF THE OLD AND NEW TESTAMENT CONTAIN A REVELATION OF THE MIND AND WILL OF GOD, AND THAT WE RECEIVE THEM AS THE RULE OF OUR FAITH AND PRACTICE?

TICE? Whether the magiſtrate has, or has not, a right to aſk us who, or what we are, can it be criminal in us to declare our common denomination and principle? Can it be criminal in us to ſay, that we are Chriſtians and Proteſtants? The ſubmitting to an unjuſt demand, does not imply an acknowledgment of the authority by which it is made. Such a demand may be honeſtly complied with, when we only teſtify a truth, in order to avoid a real evil, and to gain an important good. Beſides, the Declaration is, in reality, a diſavowal of human authority in matters of religion. It is ſo far from departing from our allegiance to our great Lord and Maſter, that it is an aſſertion of it, in the moſt explicit terms. What is it that uſually, and as Chriſtians, we mean by human authority, in matters of religion? Is it not the impoſition of Articles, Creeds, and Confeſſions, and the inſiſting upon terms of Communion, which our bleſſed Saviour hath not appointed? But by the Declaration, we renounce, and enter our proteſt againſt any ſuch claim, and ſtand up for

the

the liberty to which we are called by the Gospel.

Having, I hope, by these observations, set the conduct of the committee in a just light, I return to the objections of our common adversaries. Agreeably to their declamations against the Declaration, as indeterminate and dissatisfactory, they scarce treat us as Christians, and would insinuate that we are Deists; but I am totally at a loss to conceive what possible grounds there can be for such an insinuation. The character of Christians, and of Christian Ministers, is a character in which we rejoice and glory. That we are firm believers in the divine religion of the Son of God, appears in our discourses, appears in our writings, and, we trust, is visible our lives. Those Dissenting Ministers who have attacked several of the doctrines of the church of England, with the greatest freedom and boldness, have given undeniable proofs of their sincere faith in the Gospel, and have exerted themselves, with ability and zeal, in defence of its sacred authority. Some of the best vindications of the Christian revelation

tion have come from men, who would have sacrificed their lives rather than subscribe the Thirty-nine Articles. In fact, where are infidels more likely to be found; among the clergy of an establishment, who are invited to conformity, by the prospect of honours and rewards, or among Protestant Dissenting Ministers, who, in general, can have no motives, but conscience, and a regard to a future state, for embracing a situation exposed to many temporal inconveniences and discouragements? It would be invidious to enlarge upon this topic, but much might be said upon it, by one who is ACQUAINTED WITH THE WORLD. As to this infamous accusation of Deism, brought against the Dissenting Clergy, we might farther appeal, in confutation of it, to their numerous productions. We might appeal to the names of many persons, of respectable and eminent characters, who are now no more. We might appeal to the names of several living worthies; but Mr. Mauduit hath discussed this matter so excellently, in the conclusion of the third edition of his valuable pamphlet, that it

is

is needless to add any thing upon the subject.

Another very extraordinary charge, urged against us, is, that if we refuse to subscribe the doctrinal Articles of the church of England, as required by the Toleration Act, we cut ourselves off from the title and character of Protestants. This is really a curious discovery, which deserves, no doubt, to be treated with all the respect that is due to the quarter from whence it came. PROTESTANT CHRISTIANITY it seems, was fixed for the Dissenters at the Revolution. It was absolutely annexed to some doctrines, which, at that period, were deemed important and fundamental; and the least departure from them totally destroys our Protestantism. But what then will become of many of the established clergy, as well as of the Dissenting Ministers? A number of the established Clergy have as notoriously departed from the standard of faith, prescribed to them, as any of the Nonconformists. The Ministers of the national form of religion do, indeed, subscribe the Thirty-

Thirty-nine Articles; but that will not render them true Proteſtants, becauſe Proteſtantiſm, according to the notion lately ſtarted, conſiſts in a belief of the doctrines impoſed upon the clergy in the reign of queen Elizabeth, and upon the Diſſenters at the acceſſion of William and Mary. What havoc will this opinion make among many of the brighteſt luminaries of the church of England, and what deſtruction in the writings of thoſe who have been juſtly eſteemed the ableſt adverſaries to Popery!

But let us ſee what is the true nature of Proteſtantiſm, and what the real principles are, on which it is founded. I had always underſtood, that a Proteſtant was one who appealed to the Scriptures, as the ſole rule of faith and practice; and who rejected the abſurdities, corruptions, and abominations of the church of Rome. This I found aſſerted in a thouſand writers, and the truth of it I knew to be evident, from the whole hiſtory of the Reformation. Teſtimonies to this purpoſe might be produced, were it neceſſary, from a prodigious num-

number of valuable authors, foreign and domestic, reaching through a period of two hundred and fifty years. But I shall content myself with one late testimony, and it is a testimony which cannot but be thought decisive, as it comes from a dignitary of the establishment, whose orthodoxy hath never been called in question. I mean the truly ingenious and learned Dr. Hurd, whose beautiful critical writings, and admirable dialogues, are well known to every man of taste in this country, and who hath lately done considerable service to the cause of religion by his Introduction to the Study of Prophecy. In the twelfth sermon * he observes, that " this conclusion, that THE POPE IS " ANTICHRIST, and that other, that " THE SCRIPTURE IS THE SOLE RULE OF " CHRISTIAN FAITH, were the two " great principles on which the Re-" formation was originally founded." In the latter of these principles the Dissenters are united without a single exception; and I believe that they hold the

* Page 420, second edition.

former of them more strongly and universally than any other body of Protestants whatever.

May we not then, after what hath been produced, safely ask, whether people may not be genuine Protestants, though they do not come up to the standard of doctrines required to be subscribed by the Act of Toleration? May we not assert, that such of the non-subscribing Dissenting Ministers as are not Calvinists have a just claim to this character? We declare, in the most explicit terms, for the right of private judgment, the sufficiency of Scripture, and the sole religious authority of our Lord and Master Jesus Christ. We protest against the imposing spirit of the Church of Rome, and against all her pretensions to infallibility and dominion. We protest against her monstrous absurdities, her shameful corruptions, and her contemptible superstitions. We protest against her horrid cruelties and bloody persecutions. We protest against the claim and exercise of any similar authority over the faith and consciences of men. We

protest

protest against making the Thirty-nine Articles, or other human tests, the standards of belief, as a thing which is subversive of the essential principles of the Reformation: and, finally, we protest against the scandalous injustice of not being treated as Protestants.

As to the insinuations which are occasionally thrown out with regard to Arianism and Socinianism, it hath already been shewn that they are nothing to the purpose. They are, in fact, only the artifices of persons who want to reduce the present question, about the Extent of Toleration, to a debate concerning doctrines, with which it has not the least connexion. Arians and Socinians, according to every principle of religion and policy, have as full a right to freedom of conscience as any men, as any professing Christians whatever. It is, indeed, totally destructive of liberty to confine Toleration to certain particular tenets of the Gospel, however important these tenets may be in a religious view. When the civil magistrate thus limits his protection and indulgence to his subjects, he goes wholly out of his province: he assumes a power for which he hath no commission from the nature of his office, and the exercise of which is equally injurious to the honour of the Supreme Being, and to the happiness of mankind. It ought ever to be remembered, that God is able to maintain his own cause; and that truth only requires a fair and candid hearing in order to preserve its ground, and finally to triumph over all opposition. To assert that the fundamental doctrines of the Gospel stand in need of the aid of human laws to support them, is the highest reflection upon those doctrines. We have the assurance of our blessed Saviour, THAT THE GATES OF HELL SHALL NOT PREVAIL AGAINST HIS CHURCH*; and this is an infinitely better security than the ARM OF FLESH. It is rash and impious for men to touch, with their unhallowed hands, under the vain pretence of keeping it from being shaken, that ark of God which is sustained by almighty power; and it behoves them to reflect how highly

* Matt. xvi. 18.

offensive

offenſive ſuch a conduct muſt be to the Majeſty of heaven and earth. In fact, this maintenance of doctrines, by fines and impriſonments, by penalties and pains, inſtead of being favourable to the intereſts of truth and piety, hath been prejudicial to them in the higheſt degree. It hath been the ſource of numberleſs errors, of endleſs diviſions and animoſities, and of cruelties and perſecutions, which are an indelible diſgrace to the hiſtory of mankind.

But, in oppoſition to this juſt repreſentation of things, an alarming picture is ſet before us of the dreadful conſequences which muſt have enſued from an enlargement of the Toleration Act. The reſult of it, we are told, would have been the utmoſt diſcord and confuſion. A man, however, who hath any knowledge of the world, cannot help ſmiling at ſuch terrible apprehenſions, when there is not the leaſt ſhadow of danger. That there would not have been the leaſt ſhadow of danger hath been already determined by long experience. The liberty pleaded for hath been granted

granted by connivance; and it is allowed, that it muſt be continued to be granted in that manner. How then can that be pernicious which hath already ſubſiſted for a number of years, and which muſt, confeſſedly, ſtill ſubſiſt? The truth of the caſe is, that if our requeſt had been complied with, the conceſſion would have been followed by the moſt perfect tranquility. Had the bill paſſed both Houſes of Parliament, and received the royal aſſent, it would ſcarcely have been talked of a few days after, except to the honour of the ſtate and the church. The minds of Nonconformiſts would have been more and more conciliated to the eſtabliſhment, and leſs diſpoſed to attack it with ſeverity. The conſequences would have been entirely favourable and friendly to the public mode of religion, but not otherwiſe ſo to Diſſenting Miniſters and School-maſters, than as they would have been put into a legal ſituation.

To aſſert, however, that ſuch a ſituation is not likely to produce inconveniencies, is treated with contempt; and
it

it is thrown out that the present laws are a restraint on our passions. But let us be permitted to say that this is a mistake. The persisting to threaten, though there be no intention to strike, may irritate, but will not silence a liberal mind. I am persuaded that several of my brethren will deliver their sentiments the more freely in consequence of the obstinate refusal which hath been given to their just and reasonable request; whereas otherwise they might have been induced to hold their peace by the dictates of gratitude, and the obligations of civility and good manners. The lenity of the governors of the church might have soothed us to repose; but we will not be AWE-STRUCK by their severity. If the clergy imagine that they can affright us from an open exhibition of our opinions on every subject of religion, and on every question, in which the rights of conscience are concerned, by the vain terrors of penal laws, let them be assured, that they are totally unacquainted with our characters. If the prayer of our case had been complied with,

with, the author of the present tract, who hath been led, by inclination and duty, to the study of critical and historical learning, would probably never have engaged in any doctrinal controversy, or in any disputes with the national establishment. But he now esteems himself bound, by the most sacred ties, to appear in the injured cause of humanity and religious liberty; and hopes that he shall always be ready to embrace every proper occasion of standing up for what he apprehends to be the interests of truth, Christianity, and mankind.

Among the other evil consequences of an extended Toleration, it is insinuated, that Dissenting Ministers might become with impunity the preachers of sedition. But what ground is there for such an invidious surmise, as it is well known that they are willing to give security for their peaceable subjection to the civil magistrate? They are not disposed to bring matters of policy and government into the pulpit: and though one worthy brother*

* Mr. Radcliff.

hath

hath been provoked to throw out, in a sermon, dictated by genius and spirit, the language of manly indignation, let it be remembered that this is the result of liberty's being refused, not of its being enlarged. Our chief, I may venture to say, our sole political discourses, except on the seasons occasionally appointed by the state for public fasts and thanksgivings, are confined to the fifth of November and the first of August. On these days, we are copious in our celebration of the glorious revolution in 1688, and the happy accession of the illustrious house of Hanover in 1714. Our encomiums upon William the Third, George the First, and George the Second, are expressed with all the ardor of veneration and affection; nor are we negligent in displaying our gratitude and zeal with regard to the prince who now adorns the British throne. These things, we hope, will not be imputed to us as crimes, or be considered as objections to our enjoying the protection and favour of the present government.

But the clergy, it seems, have reason to be alarmed, lest, in the course of human events, the Dissenting Ministers should get into power; and then what would become of the Church of England? The members of it, it is intimated, might be in danger of being expelled, or even exterminated, as idolaters. If there be a likelihood of our ever rising to be formidable, wisdom and policy, perhaps, would say, that men who may possibly one day be uppermost, ought to be treated with lenity and indulgence while in a state of subjection, that they may be disposed to make suitable returns of affection and regard. But our worthy friends of the establishment may dismiss every kind of fear for two reasons. In the first place, there is no probability of our obtaining any superiority or dominion; so that the bishops and dignitaries, of the present age at least, may rest in perfect tranquillity. Secondly, if ever we should get into power, and even thought the Church of England to be idolatrous, which is by no means a general or common-mon sentiment among us, we are firmly perfuaded that Toleration ought to be extended to idolaters. In this point we have the honour of agreeing with a prelate * of diftinguifhed genius and literature; and in this point we difagree with another great prelate, though, in many refpects, we have the higheft efteem for his abilities, character, learning, and writings †.

It is farther objected to the late application, that only a fmall number of Minifters were concerned in it, fo that, in reality, it might be confidered as afking a favour, which may almoft be called perfonal. The beft anfwer to this reprefentation of things is briefly to mention a few plain facts. At a meeting of the general body of the three denominations of Prefbyterians, Independents, and Antipædobaptifts, in and about London, held at the Library in Red-crofs-ftreet, March 4th, 1772, fifty being prefent, it was re-

* Dr. Warburton, bifhop of Gloucefter.
† Dr. Lowth, bifhop of Oxford.

solved, That the taking off the Subscription required of Proteſtant Diſſenting Miniſters, and the obtaining relief for Tutors and School-maſters, are very deſirable and important objects; that application ſhould be made to Parliament for theſe purpoſes; and that a committee be choſen to manage the affair, with power to ſummon the general body as they ſhould ſee occaſion. To theſe reſolutions only one perſon diſagreed. On the following day, about twenty other miniſters met at the Library, and expreſſed to the chairman of the committee their approbation of, and concurrence with the deſign; nor do I recollect that the original vote hath been impugned at any ſubſequent aſſembly, by the few who have appeared the moſt diſſatisfied with the conduct of the committee. The approved miniſters of the three denominations, in and about London, are ninety-five. Beſides thoſe who concurred from the beginning in the application to Parliament, there were others who appeared on the ſame ſide of the queſtion at ſucceeding meetings; and

ſeve-

several, who by age, illness, or various circumstances, were prevented from attending at all, have given undoubted proofs of their hearty assent to the scheme. It happened, indeed, that, during the prosecution of the affair, a small number objected to the management of the committee. One gentleman disliked the having of any Declaration at all, as being an improper concession to the state in matters of religion. Others were displeased that the Declaration precluded an open profession before the civil magistrate of their firm belief of the doctrinal articles of the Church of England; nor did they approve of the Testimonial required by the bill, apprehending it might be converted to the prejudice of some worthy men of the Methodistical stamp, who, though not regularly admitted among us, might desire to qualify under the character of Dissenting Ministers; an apprehension which, to me, appears not to have the least foundation. Be that as it may, it is certain that, on no account, in no question whatever, were there more hands held up than six in the way of opposition;

an union this, which, I believe, hath not been found in any other meafure of fo public a nature; to which may be added, that there is not a fingle perfon in the body, who profeffes to wifh that his brethren, who lie under difficulties with regard to the Toleration Act, may be left fubject to its penalties.

This great unanimity is by no means confined to the Diffenting Clergy in or near the city of London. The juft and important reafons which determined the Minifters of the metropolis and of the places adjacent, to take up the matter fomewhat fuddenly, and late in the feffion of Parliament, prevented that univerfal application to their brethren in the country, which was originally intended; but the members of the committee, and other perfons, had an opportunity of applying to a confiderable number of them in different parts of the kingdom, and received, in return, their entire approbation and hearty encouragement. Many of their letters might be produced to this purpofe; and it appeared by ftriking facts how zealous they
were

were in the cause. The most agreeable proofs have since been transmitted of their uniting with us in the same wishes, and of their having the same sentiments with regard to the propriety of an application for the removal of Subscription. Should, therefore, a second application to Parliament be thought adviseable, it will be fully seen how universally the Dissenting Ministers in England and Wales are solicitous for an enlargement of the Toleration Act, and how entirely they approve of proper measures being taken to effect so desirable and important an object. The laity have manifested, likewise, their zeal in the cause, though immediately interested in that part alone of the late bill, which was intended to provide for the free education of their children, and which, indeed, is a matter of great importance to the whole body of Nonconformists.

But were it a fact, that only a minority of the Dissenting Ministers had solicited relief in the matter of Subscription, this ought not to have been an hindrance to their success. Their cause rests on its own
rea-

reasonableness and equity, independent of numbers. The grievance is personal, and therefore every single man hath a right to seek redress. He hath a title too, on the principles of justice and sound policy, to be heard, and attended to, in his petition. The arguments in favour of a liberal Toleration apply to all, however few, who cannot conscientiously subscribe Tests of human composition,

With regard to the very small number of Ministers who were unfriendly to their brethren in the late affair, and endeavoured to obstruct the solicited relief, let me be permitted to give them a hint for the regulation of their future conduct. It behoves them to take care, that they do not inadvertently injure themselves. The time is probably approaching when the Thirty-nine Articles will be revised and altered. A scheme of this kind is in agitation among the governors of the church; and should it be carried into execution, there can be little doubt but that strict Calvinism will be excluded, and an Arminian turn be given to the established doctrines.

trines. In that case, a number of Dissenting Ministers, who are zealous Calvinists, may labour under similar difficulties with those who now object to particular parts of the present Articles. They may be obliged by law to subscribe opinions which they apprehend to be contrary to the truth of the Gospel, and, in order to obtain relief, may wish for the assistance of their brethren who are in different sentiments. Nor need they be afraid of a retaliation; for all possible aid will, I doubt not, be granted them, upon the great principles which unite the whole body of the Dissenters*.

* Should the projected Reformation of the Church of England be carried into execution, among other difficulties attending the undertaking, one will undoubtedly be, how to settle the laws with respect to Protestant Dissenting Ministers. Must they accommodate their consciences to the fluctuations of the public opinion, and be obliged to subscribe Articles different from, perhaps contrary to those imposed upon them before? or will they be entirely freed from the burden of human impositions? I hope that it will not be found so easy to enact new penal statutes in matters of religion, as it hath been to retain the old ones.

It is in vain, however, to attempt the removal of particular objections to the extension of the Toleration Act, since we are told, that the " nature and design of civil society are clearly AGAINST us."

In answer to this bold and groundless position, it is sufficient to assert, that the nature and design of civil society are clearly FOR us: but if any clergyman be disposed to rest the cause on a fair, full, and distinct discussion of the point, some or other of my brethren will, I doubt not, undertake it with pleasure. Indeed, the farther consideration of the question is needless, because it hath already been determined in the immortal writings of Locke, Hoadly, and other friends to civil and religious liberty. It is the intention of every just and well formed system of government to protect its subjects in the exercise of their most sacred rights, among which the right of worshipping God according to the dictates of conscience, is essential and unalienable. To say, therefore, that the nature and design of civil society are clearly against repealing the pe-

penalties of the Toleration Act, if it be said with sincerity, can only be the result of uncommon ignorance.

In support of a doctrine so contrary to every principle of reason, religion, and sound policy, it is alledged that "the state hath an undoubted right to control overt acts, and that preaching is an overt act of some importance to the state." But has the meaning of an overt act been attended to in this assertion? According to the idea here given of it, it might be extended to almost every circumstance in human life. The transactions of individuals in their nearest and dearest private concerns, in the management of their affairs, the regulation of their families, the education of their children, and a thousand particulars besides, may be considered, in their tendencies and effects, as important to the community. But are these things to be controlled by penal laws? In that case, personal and domestic liberty and happiness, on which public felicity is founded, would be totally destroyed, and, by consequence, every thing which renders our present existence valuable and delightful.

The true and proper notion of an overt act is an act done with a malicious intention, an act criminally injurious to the public, and which can be proved to be such by just and legal evidence. This I apprehend is the sense of the word, as it occurs in law-books, and as it is used in judicial proceedings. In this sense of the word, the civil magistrate hath not only an undoubted authority, but it is a prime part of his business, to control overt acts; and here may be drawn the line of Toleration. Whatever religious principles any man may pretend to, whatever pleas of conscience may be urged by him, if he hurts his neighbour in person or property, if he disturbs his fellow-creatures in the exercise of their rights and privileges, he ought to be restrained and punished. This is the precise point at which it becomes the duty of the state to interfere; and if the state should interfere sooner, and extend its jurisdiction to the tendencies of opinions, it will be impossible

sible to know where to stop. Speculations and fancies about the tendencies of opinions might be carried on to the entire destruction of Toleration, and the vindication of every species of persecution and tyranny. An over-zealous Arminian will be ready to contend, that several doctrines are contained even in the Thirty-nine Articles of the Church of England, which are calculated to have a bad effect on the morals and happiness of mankind. An over-zealous Calvinist will as warmly plead, that the power ascribed to man by some divines, and other tenets held by them, are extremely prejudicial to the interests of holiness. Things of this kind are too apt to be thrown out on both sides, which have a stronger tincture of passion than of reason. Accusations of the like sort might be produced against a variety of religious sentiments, till, at length, not liberty only, but piety and charity, would be lost in the contest. But I say the less on the subject, as my ingenious and valuable friend, Dr. Furneaux, who hath been particularly attacked upon it, will do ample justice

justice to himself and to the cause in which he is engaged.

I shall leave it to the same gentleman to vindicate himself and the Protestant Dissenters, with regard to what is alleged against him and them, concerning the design of appointing bishops in America. The charge of holding intolerant principles upon this head is unfair in the highest degree; for such principles are disclaimed and abhorred by the whole body of Protestant Dissenters. With respect to the American Episcopalians, if they ask for a bishop as a religious officer, to ORDAIN, CONFIRM, and perform the other SPIRITUAL duties belonging to that character, they have a right to be indulged in their request; and to deny that they have such a right would be a departure from the fundamental Ideas of Toleration. Should it, therefore, be thought needful to send bishops to the colonies, who shall have no power or prerogative, OF ANY KIND, that may be detrimental to their fellow Christians, and who shall only be put on a fair and equal footing with every
dis-

different sect in matters of religion and conscience, such an institution ought not to be opposed, and will not, I am persuaded, be opposed by the Dissenters in England. Neither ought it to be objected to barely on account of suspicions, jealousies, and surmises, that it may be converted to the prejudice of the liberty of others, provided a reasonable security be given that this shall not be the case. If the scheme hath any view to the obtaining for the Church of England such an ascendency and dominion in America as shall be injurious to the privileges of the religious bodies of men already settled there, which I would by no means insinuate, the affair may safely be left to be adjusted between the government and the colonists themselves. Let me, however, be permitted to add, that if the Americans have entertained groundless prejudices on the subject, the conduct of the English bishops, with regard to the late bill, hath not been at all calculated to remove them.

Having gone through the principal objections to the MATTER of our application,

tion, it will be neceffary briefly to confider the MANNER in which it has been carried on, becaufe this, likewife, is pretended to be very improper and indefenfible. Indeed, if the object, on account of which we had recourfe to Legiflature, was altogether unreafonable, it is of little importance to enquire how it was conducted, fince, in that cafe, no prudence or delicacy of behaviour ought to have been of any avail in our behalf. On the other hand, if our petition was, IN ITSELF, moft juftifiable and equitable, fome little irregularities in the mode of urging it ought not to have been converted to its prejudice. But let us fee what the improprieties were which reflected fuch a difgrace on the MANNER of our application.

One accufation is, that the committee PERSONALLY applied to members of Parliament in favour of the bill. It is true, that they did fo, and they were fully juftified in fuch a conduct. They had a right to reprefent their cafe to the perfons who would condefcend to hear it; nor was there, by that means, an undue influence

ence exerted. The Diffenting Ministers did not directly folicit any member's vote: they did not attempt to move his paffions, or to lay a reftraint upon his confcience. They only begged that noblemen and gentlemen would give their prefence in the Houfe, and their attention to the fubject. They only requefted a fair and candid hearing of their caufe, and that the Peers and Reprefentatives of the People would act agreeably to what fhould appear to be juft and equitable, after fuch a hearing of the queftion before them. The committee were ready, likewife, to anfwer, as far as lay in their power, any queftions which might be propofed to them, or to remove any difficulties that might lie in the minds of the great and refpectable men on whom they had the honour of waiting. All this might be done in almoft every cafe, and it might reafonably be done in our particular cafe. If, therefore, there was any impropriety in this part of our conduct, it is an impropriety which muft be repeated on a future occafion.

But we are told, that the Manner in which the Diffenting Ministers carried on their

their application to Parliament was, in another respect, still more strikingly indefensible: "Letters were sent from persons in "the country to their representatives ear- "nestly requesting their votes." How far votes were directly sollicited I am not able to say, not having seen any letters of that kind; but, with regard to the having of recourse to members of Parliament, and even asking their support of the bill, I shall not scruple to assert, that it is capable of an entire justification. Who are the gentlemen with whom the Dissenters are usually connected, and in whose favour they exert their influence at the time of an election? They are, undoubtedly, such gentlemen as are understood to be the known and approved friends of civil and religious liberty. When, therefore, a question arose of great importance to the rights of conscience in general, and to the Nonconformists in particular, it was natural for Dissenters, it was their duty, to apply to those representatives whom they believed to be friendly to their cause, and whose concurrence and aid they had a title to hope for and expect. It might otherwise wife have been thought, that they did not wish for an extension of the Act of Toleration.

I will go farther, and say, that such members of Parliament as refused their assistance to the late bill ought not to be encouraged by Dissenters at any future election. The gentlemen who were averse to our cause might be honest men, who acted under the direction of a misguided conscience. I have no doubt but that this was the case with regard to the most zealous of our adversaries in the House of Commons: but such gentlemen must excuse me in saying, that those who will oppose the repeal of unjust and inhuman penal statutes must be very improper and insufficient guardians of the public liberty, and especially of the liberties of the people who are affected by those statutes. For my own part, I have no hesitation in declaring, that I would not, on any account, give my vote for a representative who hath refused to concur in improving the Toleration Act; and I think myself fully vindicable in this resolution. A man of such narrow principles can never be considered

sidered, by genuine Dissenters, as worthy to be entrusted with the protection of the privileges of a free nation. A friend to intolerance, if he be really such from the dictates of his understanding, must be destitute of wisdom; if he adopts the character from motives of interest or ambition, he must be destitute of integrity and humanity: and surely it must be justifiable to deny our encouragement to persons who are deficient in such important and essential qualifications for a seat in the Legislature, as wisdom, integrity, and humanity.

In fact, the declamation about the impropriety of applying to members of Parliament is futile to the last degree. Such an application must be made, in cases whether of a PARTIAL or a GENERAL good. It is honourable to plead in an honourable cause. The present course of the world requires a conduct of this kind, and the most equitable business cannot otherwise be transacted. With regard to the Dissenting Committee, the liberty we took of personally waiting upon noblemen and gentlemen, was not at the hazard of our

our INGENUOUS CHARACTERS. It was peculiarly neceffary, as our views and principles were not fufficiently known. It was proper to explain them, becaufe they required only to be explained, in order to fet the reafonablenefs of our petition in a clear and ftriking point of view. This, indeed, is the circumftance which feems to have rendered our vifits to the members of Parliament particularly difagreeable to the enemies of the bill.

HÆRET LATERI—ARUNDO.
But as the wound is fo flight, as the ARUNDO is not LETHALIS, there is the lefs occafion for fo much offence being taken.

After all, was there no influence, no power exerted on the other fide of the queftion? Is it true, that the Diffenting Minifters had nothing to contend with but the ARGUMENTS WHICH MIGHT OCCUR AGAINST THEM? In this cafe, they would have thought themfelves engaged in a very favourable conteft. Were not the Bifhops able to apply to all ranks of men with a weight which could not poffi-bly be exerted on our part? Could they not, by the advantage of their eminent

ftation,

station, have immediate recourse to every temporal Lord? Have they not an easy access to the highest personal authority in this kingdom? And did they really continue totally inactive, trusting solely to the goodness of their cause.*? Did they not speak to a single Peer? Did they not go FARTHER? Was there no influence reaching upwards to the very SUMMIT OF POWER, and then descending with great force against us? Will any man lay his hand upon his heart, and say, that it was the mere rectitude of continuing the penal laws against the Nonconformists which brought down the whole weight of government upon us in the House of Lords? It is true, that we are simple men, who are precluded, by our situation, from much knowledge of the world: but, ignorant as we are, this is one of the CREDENDA, which our faith will never be able to digest. An inhabitant of the ULTIMA

---

* Facts might here be mentioned; but the author purposely declines insisting upon them. Should the charge of having endeavoured to exert an undue influence be renewed against the Dissenting Ministers, the conduct of their opponents may perhaps hereafter, be more fully considered.

THULE,

Thule, if he had but an opportunity of perusing sometimes an English news-paper, would be incapable of believing, that a majority of British Peers, could, in the year 1772, be induced, by reason and argument ONLY, to display their zeal against the repealing of statutes which are a reproach to justice, to religion, and to humanity.

As the Protestant Dissenting Ministers have conducted themselves so imprudently in the late affair, they are advised to return quietly to their studies and ministerial labours. It is with pleasure that they engage in the more immediate business of their profession, and they wish to be drawn from it as little as possible. When, however, they are called out of the common line of duty by some great occasion, interesting to Christianity and mankind, they think themselves amply justified in stepping forth with alacrity into a wider field of action; but it is not their ambition to go farther out of their accustomed limits, or to continue longer in a situation which does not usually belong to them, than necessity and honour may

may demand. Let them be indulged in their requeſt for legal ſecurity and protection, and they will thankfully retire to their private employments. They do not deſire to be troubleſome to men of rank, or to haunt the levees of the great. If they can obtain a Toleration which is ſettled on the ſolid baſis of law, and not held by the precarious tenure of connivance and compaſſion, they will have nothing more to aſk of the ſtate.

This may ſerve as an anſwer to thoſe perſons who imagine that the Diſſenting Clergy had aims beyond the objects of their late application to Parliament. It is not true, that they had any farther deſigns. Their ſole purpoſes were to be delivered from the burden of Subſcription, and to procure relief for Tutors and School-maſters; and they had not the moſt diſtant thoughts of applying hereafter for privileges and benefits of a different nature. The ſuppoſition that they were actuated by ambitious views, is grounded on an ignorance of their characters and intentions. They were animated ly no regard to the honours and profits

of

of the present world. Their ambition is to go on quietly and securely in worshipping God agreeably to the dictates of their consciences; and if they can be serviceable, by their labours and their writings, to the cause of religion or of literature, it is the highest glory to which they aspire.

The last instance of impropriety charged upon the Dissenting Ministers, is their CHOICE OF THE TIME IN WHICH THE APPLICATION TO PARLIAMENT WAS MADE. The TIME, however, is a consideration that ought not to be attended to, when any thing is solicited which is a matter of right. In that case, redress ought, in duty, to be granted at the instant in which it is asked. It never can be too soon to do what is always essentially right and fit to be done. It never can be an improper season for expunging penal laws from the statute book which are a disgrace to legislature and to humanity. The only real objection that can be urged against the Time of the late application is, that it was not made before; that laws have been so long acquiesced in which are unjust and barbarous, and the repeal of which

which ought to have taken place from the earliest period wherein it was seen that the execution of them was contrary to every principle worthy of men or of Christians.

But it is said, that the Church had already been attacked by the Clergy's Petition, by the Nullum Tempus Bill, and by the Quaker's Bill. Were we to admit that these things were unjustifiable attacks upon the national establishment of religion, (and how far they were so I am not capable of judging in the two last cases, as not having attended to them) what connection have they with the affair of the Dissenters? The request of the Dissenting Ministers was, in no view, an act of hostility against the Church of England. She had, properly speaking, no concern in the question, nor could she be injured by its being determined in their favour. Was it an attack upon the Church of England, to endeavour to free the British constitution of government from intolerant laws and a persecuting spirit? Was it an attack upon the Church of England, to solicit the removal of of penalties which she HERSELF owns cannot be carried into execution? The very supposition is the severest reflection upon her that her most inveterate enemies could suggest. Had the Bishops been fortunate enough to have seen the Dissenting Clergy's application in a favourable light, they might have had the glory of giving a reputation to the religious establishment of this kingdom which hath never been obtained by any religious establishment in Christendom. They might have wiped off the reproach of having it asserted, that Toleration is more perfect, and scriptural Christianity upon a better footing in Turky than in any other country of Europe. They might have had the power of appealing to their enemies, and of saying, that the Church of England had discovered such a decisive mark of her being the true church of our blessed Saviour, as no Christian, no Protestant nation besides could afford. It would have been, as a great * prelate hath expressed it, THE SEAL OF THE LIVING GOD UPON HER.

* Dr. Warburton.

With regard to the Time in general of applying to Parliament for an enlargement of the Toleration Act, what could be a more proper one than the present? Are we likely to have hereafter a more just and more gracious Prince? Are we likely to find a milder and more liberal bench of Prelates? Are we likely to meet with a period, which, upon the whole, will be less favourable to persecution? Certainly, such a state of things was the very season in which the Dissenting Ministers might hope and expect to obtain a compliance with their very reasonable petition. It would be too late for them to ask relief, should evil days approach, and government become unequitable and ungenerous. They gave the best proof of their good opinion of, and of their good disposition to, the state, by making their application at this particular juncture; and, whatever narrow politicians may think, the admission of their claim would have been honourable and advantageous to the public.

The

The Impropriety of the Time is the common topic of statesmen and of churchmen, when they are unwilling to grant a reasonable request: but it is unworthy of being mentioned by an ingenuous mind, especially when the request is founded on the great principles of truth and humanity. A topic it is, which hath so often been insisted upon, that it is become disgraceful, and carries with it an idea of contempt and ridicule.

But after all the insinuations thrown out against the Dissenting Ministers; after all the objections to the MATTER, the MANNER, and the TIME of their late application; after all the suggestions of their disbelief of fundamental doctrines; after all the invidious hints at the dangerous principles supposed to be held by them, it is acknowledged that they are very worthy men; and some of them, it is said, if they were conformists to the established church, would ADORN ANY STATION WHICH MIGHT FALL TO THEIR LOT. They cannot but be flattered, that so favourable an opinion should at last be entertained of them: nor are they so insensible of the advantages of life, as not to think it desirable to partake of the emoluments of the national form of worship, provided they could do it consistently with the preservation of a good conscience. But they must be permitted to say, that the Church hath not taken the proper method of inviting them to enter into her communion. They are persuaded, with the eminent bishop Warburton, that no religious establishment can be vindicated, but upon the footing of its being connected with an equal and an extensive Toleration; and while the religious establishment of this country continues averse to such a Toleration, they are obliged, in honour and duty, to remain separated from it. So long as the Church of England retains the very essence of Popery, by contending for the subsistence of penal laws, in matters that relate only to conscience, and the interests of another world; they imagine that they hear the voice of God speaking to them in his word, " Come out of her, my people." Whereas, if she were willing

to

to grant a free indulgence to all who differ from her, many Diffenting Ministers would be better difpofed to unite with her, when certain alterations are made in the terms of her admiffion, and in the modes and forms of her difcipline and worfhip.

The determined oppofition of the Bifhops to the requeft of the Proteftant Diffenting Clergy might afford room for many obfervations. The fubject is capable of being confidered in a variety of refpects, which would not, perhaps, exhibit the conduct of their Lordfhips in fo favourable a light as a candid and liberal mind might wifh to put it in; but I have no inclination to enlarge upon a difagreeable and invidious topic. Whatever may be my fentiments with regard to the part they acted in the late affair, I am not infenfible that, in general, they are men of decent and amiable characters, and of foft and gentle manners. Some of them are eminent for their talents in bufinefs: others of them are diftinguifhed ornaments of the republic of literature, and have done fignal fervice to the caufe of Chriftianty.

I re-

I recollect that a Pearce, a Warburton, a Lowth, a Law, a Newton, and a Mofs, have a feat on the Epifcopal Bench; and I wifh that all who belong to that bench may obtain a reputation that fhall be fixed on the moft folid bafis. Should, therefore, a fecond application be made to Parliament, I hope that the venerable body of Prelates will candidly and fully reconfider the matter. I hope that they will reconfider it, not according to the principles of a narrow and miftaken policy, but in the grand points of view which alone are worthy of their attention and their character. The queftions with them ought to be, and, I truft, will be, what are the dictates of true Chriftianity on the fubject; what are the demands of a juft and equitable Toleration; and what are the directions of that found wifdom " which " is from above, which looks not at the " things which are feen and temporal, but " at the things which are unfeen and eter- " nal;" their Lordfhips, I flatter myfelf, will keep in mind the admirable words of the earl of Chatham, that, " in this free " coun-

"country, twenty benches of Bishops
"ought not to set law and humanity at
"variance." They will remember, I am
persuaded, that, in order to shew their real
liberality of sentiment, and their real aversion to persecution, it is not sufficient for
us to be told, as we often are, that they
are mild and tolerant in their spirit and
temper; for our Saviour hath left another
criterion from which to judge of the dispositions of men, when he saith, "By
"their fruits ye shall know them." The
Bishops have not only a political, but a
CHRISTIAN character to maintain; and
the CHRISTIAN character is infinitely the
most important. The Christian character
alone it is which will be of any avail,
when all human splendors shall cease;
when the humble Nonconformist teacher
and the exalted prelate will be no otherwise distinguished, than as they distinguished themselves upon earth, by their
conscientious adherence to truth and integrity.

Though the Protestant Dissenting Ministers have been unsuccessful in their endeavours

P

deavours to obtain a juft enlargement of Chriftian Toleration, they have no reafon to look back upon their conduct with difapprobation or regret. On the contrary, they have caufe for rejoicing in the part they have acted. They have difcharged that duty which they owed to themfelves, to their people, and pofterity. They have entered their public proteft againft laws which are injurious to their juft rights, as men and as Chriftians. They have obtained the verdict of the Britifh Houfe of Commons in their favour. They have had the concurrence and fupport of the moft honourable and illuftrious characters in this country; and the general voice of the public hath approved of their proceedings. Their upright principles and views have been better known than they ever were before; and, with regard to the Diffenting intereft in particular, which they believe to be the intereft of fcriptural Chriftianity, it hath, perhaps, been more promoted by the denial, than it would have been by the grant of their petition. Perhaps, it has fared no worfe with Chriftianity,

tianity, that she has always had the secular arm against her, as it is at this day; and that she has never yet been, I say not established, but even legally tolerated, in any country of Christendom.

The providence of God does not always accomplish its ends in the manner which may seem the most desirable to weak and fallible men. The opposition that is made to the cause of truth and righteousness is often the very circumstance which renders it, in the final result of things, more illustriously conspicuous, and more completely victorious. Were slight concessions made as soon as asked, mankind would much longer be contented with a partial and defective reformation. But that timid and sinister policy, which sets itself against the smallest degree of alteration and improvement, defeats its own purposes. It occasions the spirit of enquiry to be pushed much farther than was originally intended. This spirit gains strength by resistance, till, at length, it breaks through the barriers erected against it by bigotry, intolerance, and worldly cunning. The period will come,

come, in which penal ftatutes, in matters that belong to confcience and to God, will be difmiffed with univerfal abhorrence: and when BIOGRAPHY fhall relate, in future ages, the eminent virtues and the learned labours of fome of the prefent bench of Bifhops, fhe will, at the fame time, be obliged to record it with fhame, as an aftonifhing blot in their characters, that they were capable of pleading for the continuance of laws, which are repugnant to every dictate of wifdom, every precept of the Gofpel, and every fentiment of humanity.

FINIS.

www.ingramcontent.com/pod-product-compliance
Lightning Source LLC
Chambersburg PA
CBHW020140170426
43199CB00010B/827